*Leader's Guide*

# *Guided Meditations on God's Reign*

A QUIET PLACE APART

*Leader's Guide*

# *Guided Meditations on God's Reign: Benevolence, Kingdom Now, Sharing, New Jerusalem*

*Jane E. Ayer*

*Saint Mary's Press*
*Christian Brothers Publications*
*Winona, Minnesota*

Genuine recycled paper with 10% post-consumer waste.
Printed with soy-based ink.

The publishing team for this book included Brian Singer-Towns, development editor; Rebecca Fairbank, copy editor; Gabrielle Koenig, production editor; Cären Yang, cover designer; cover photo by Digital Imagery, copyright © 2000 by PhotoDisc, Inc.; produced by the graphics division of Saint Mary's Press.

The scriptural text throughout this book is freely adapted. These adaptations are not to be interpreted or used as official translations of the Scriptures.

The acknowledgments continue on page 50.



Printed in the United States of America

Printing: 9 8 7 6 5 4 3 2 1

Year: 2009 08 07 06 05 04 03 02 01

ISBN 0-88489-703-6

Library of Congress Cataloging-in-Publication Data

Ayer, Jane E.
Guided meditations on God's reign: benevolence, kingdom now, sharing, New Jerusalem / Jane E. Ayer.
p. cm.—(A quiet place apart)
ISBN 0-88489-703-6 (pbk.)
1. Bible—Meditations. 2. Christian life—Biblical teaching. I. Title.
BS680.C47 A94 2000
242'.5—dc21

2001001499

# *Contents*

*To Andre,*
*my incredible grandson,*
*because of you*
*the Reign of God*
*is more wonderfully tangible.*

*I love you as high as the sky.*

# *Directions for Leading the Meditations*

**LEADER PREPARATION** As the meditation leader, you will find that preparation is especially important to the success of a guided meditation. Pray the meditation before leading a group in it. This will help you to become comfortable with its style and content. Some materials may require a brief doctrinal review with the group. By praying the meditation first, you will become aware if there is a need for that.

If you choose to have your group do one of the optional art expressions as a follow-up to the meditation, it is best if you try it out before the group gathers to make sure it works well and to know better what directions to give.

If you intend to guide the meditations yourself rather than use the accompanying recording, rehearse the guided prayer, including the introductory comments, the scriptural reading, and the opening and closing prayers, so that appropriate and sufficient time is allowed for the imagery to take place and for prayerful reflection to occur. The meditations should be read slowly and prayerfully, using soft instrumental music as a background.

Only a good reader who has prepared should read aloud the scriptural passage that precedes each guided meditation. The scriptural passage is important to establishing the theme and the tone of the meditation. Read it with reverence and expression, using a Bible.

**PARTICIPANT PREPARATION** To introduce praying a guided meditation, it might be helpful to explain that the participants will be using a prayer form that will call upon their imagination, and that the Holy Spirit graces our imagination during prayer to help us communicate with God. Remember that this type of prayer may not be easy for everyone in the group. Some may be self-conscious about closing their eyes; some may have difficulty getting in touch with their feelings; some may have personal obstacles in their relationship with God. Sometimes it helps to reassure the participants that if they cannot "get into it," they can use the quiet time to just slow themselves down, relax, and talk to the Lord in their own way. Participants can also be told that although the meditation is guided, if the Spirit leads them in another direction, it is okay for them to go with their own reflection and not worry about the words being spoken. Be gentle, let go, and let the Spirit work.

A possible difficulty, one that may not be apparent at first, may be encountered by those who wear the type of contact lenses that prevent them from closing their eyes for an extended period of time. Invite these participants to put their head down, hiding their eyes in the dark crook of their arm, if they are unable to remove the lenses. Another possible difficulty may be experienced by those who have a sinus problem or asthma. Instead of breathing through their nose during the deep-breathing exercises, they can breathe quietly through their mouth.

**MUSIC** Quiet instrumental music is important for setting and keeping the mood of the meditation. Music can be playing even as the group gathers. It is a nice background for giving instructions. Have additional tapes or compact discs ready to play during the activities after the guided meditation. Ideally, the follow-up activities will take place in a separate space; therefore, it is less disruptive if cassette or CD players are already set up in the different areas.

**REFLECTION QUESTIONS** Allowing time for the participants to reflect and to name the experiences that they have just gone through is a necessary part of these prayer experiences. The reflection questions will help the participants do this successfully. Choose several reflection questions (or use questions similar to them) and type them up, leaving room after each for a response. Make a copy for each participant. Allow enough time for each person to respond to the questions and to share his or her responses with the group. These prayer experiences are not meant to be rushed.

To avoid disrupting the quiet mood of the meditation time, pass out the reflection questions (facedown) as the participants take their places. Also, give a pen or pencil to each person. If people are sitting on the floor, you could hand out hardcover books or clipboards to facilitate writing. Explain that you are distributing reflection questions for use after the meditation.

Assure the participants that their responses are private and that their papers are not going to be collected. When it is time for sharing, honor and affirm all responses, and respect those persons who do not wish to answer aloud.

**ART EXPRESSION AND PRAYER RITUAL (OPTIONAL)**

Each prayer experience comes with two or three optional art expressions, each containing a prayer ritual. You might choose to use one of these rather than the reflection questions, as participants tend to share more readily with something meaningful and tangible in their hands.

If you choose to do an optional art expression, prepare the art materials ahead of time and lay them out in the area where the participants will work. Familiarize the group with the art activity before the prayer time, if possible, so as not to disrupt the meditative mood during the experience. This should allow you to give particular directions for the art activity without having to answer a lot of questions. If you have previously completed the art expression, it might be helpful to show your sample artwork at this time.

**SETTING**

It is imperative that the area for the prayer experience be quiet—no ringing of telephones, bells, and the like. If necessary, put a sign on the outside of your door: Praying! Please do not disturb!

Participants may sit in chairs or find a comfortable position on the floor, but they must be three or four feet from one another so that they each have their own space and do not distract one another. Therefore, the area must be large enough so the participants are not crowded. Lying down on the floor should be discouraged, as some participants are likely to fall asleep.

**CENTERPIECE (OPTIONAL)**

The theme of each prayer experience can be enhanced by creating a centerpiece that can be placed on a small table, an altar, or the middle of the floor. The centerpiece should include objects that reflect the message of the prayer. For example, for the meditation on benevolence ("Breath of All Life"), you might display framed art or sculptures that depict various beautiful elements of creation (nature, persons, animals, etc.) as well as artwork that depicts parts of creation that have been polluted or forsaken. Include candles and a Bible opened to the scriptural passage, all decoratively arranged on a gold or purple cloth.

A centerpiece for the meditation on Kingdom now ("The Spirit of the Lord Has Sent Me") might include a scroll with the Scripture passage printed on it; placards that read "the poor, the blind, the prisoner"; or a collage of pictures representative of the poor, the blind, or the imprisoned; candles; and a Bible opened to the scriptural passage, all displayed on an earth-tone cloth.

To set the theme for the meditation on sharing ("Everything in Common"), the centerpiece might display a toy train, money, food, possessions (such as designer clothes), candles, and a Bible opened to the scriptural passage, all attractively arranged on a green or tan cloth.

To enhance the meditation on New Jerusalem ("God's Name on Your Forehead"), the centerpiece might consist of a trumpet, gold or shimmering fabric, a placard containing the words "God's name on my forehead," a large pillar candle, and a Bible opened to the scriptural passage, all positioned decoratively on a white cloth.

**MATERIALS NEEDED**

- a Bible
- an audiotape or CD player
- the meditation recording or script

- tapes or CDs of instrumental music
- reflection questions (a copy for each participant)
- pens or pencils
- clipboards or hardcover books to facilitate writing, if needed
- materials for the art expression (optional; see individual project's needs)
- a centerpiece to reflect the theme (optional)
- a sign that reads Praying! Please do not disturb! (if necessary)

# *Benevolence*
# *Breath of All Life*

This reflective prayer experience, "Breath of All Life," is based on the Creation account in Genesis, which expresses clearly all that God lovingly and magnanimously intended. It reminds us that we are the heirs of both the beauty and the responsibility of God's benevolence in this wonderful gift of creation.

THEME After you have given directions to the participants and set the tone for meditation, introduce the theme by saying something like the following:

> God has granted us the incredible gift and responsibility to both benefit from and care for our earth and surrounding universe. We often ignore or neglect this awesome responsibility. We need to examine how well we support the care of God's creation and discover ways we can be more attentive and improve in our caregiving of Mother Earth. By entering our quiet place apart, we will allow ourselves to get in touch with our God-given role as faithful and caring stewards of all creation.

OPENING Read aloud this opening prayer:

> Creator God, you have blessed us with the richness of your creation, and we give you thanks and praise for desiring to share it with us. We know we have often failed to care for your gifts around us, and so we come to you today in our quiet place apart, asking for your guiding presence to help us be better caretakers of our universe. Grant us the grace during this prayer experience to examine how we have been faithful and unfaith-

> ful in the tending of your creation. Guide us to make positive changes in the way we receive and look after your gifts. We lift these thoughts up to you, our loving Creator God. Amen.

**SCRIPTURE** Read aloud Genesis 1:26—2:4, using a Bible.

**SCRIPT** Play the "Breath of All Life" meditation on the accompanying recording, or slowly and reverently read aloud the following script for the guided meditation. Play soft, instrumental background music:

> Today you will enter the hush of your quiet place and meet Jesus in your imagination. First, you will begin by doing some deep-breathing exercises. When I say to, if you can, breathe in and out through your nose very quietly during these exercises. Close your eyes and get comfortable. You will be relaxing your entire body.
>
> Breathe in deeply . . . hold it . . . breathe out slowly and completely. Breathe in deeply . . . hold it . . . breathe out slowly and completely. Again, breathe in deeply . . . hold it . . . breathe out slowly and completely.
>
> Allow your feet and ankles to relax. . . . Relax your legs . . . and your hips. . . . Stay mindful of your breathing. Relax your stomach muscles . . . and now your chest. . . . Just relax. . . . Let your arms grow limp. . . . Relax your wrists, . . . your hands, . . . and your fingers. . . . Keep breathing in deeply and out slowly.
>
> Allow your shoulders to become heavy. . . . Let all the tension drain from your shoulders. . . . Relax your neck, . . . your facial muscles, . . . your forehead, . . . and even your eyelids. . . . Just relax. . . . Breathe in deeply . . . hold it . . . breathe out slowly and completely. [Pause.]

Today you are visiting a fabulous art museum. You are safely alone and open to the beauty and the messages of the artwork which surrounds you. Wall after wall displays oils, watercolors, pencil sketches, ink drawings, and more. Pillars and shelves hold sculptures and statues. It is peaceful here. Walk into the first section. It is completely about nature. Scenes of waterfalls, sunsets, ocean tides, rainbows, winter storms, morning dew, meadow, woods, mountains, glaciers, rain forest, gardens, and every other place in nature decorate the walls. Walk along until you find your favorite place in nature. . . . What is it of? What does it say to you? How does it make you feel? Take a moment to thank God for this place in nature that you love. [Pause.]

Move along into the next room. Animals, reptiles, insects, birds, and fish adorn the walls or stand freely in marble, bronze, wood, or glass. Take time to look at everything. Pick out a few of God's creatures that delight you or intrigue you. And take a moment to thank God for all that is good. [Pause.]

Enter the third room. Portraits and photographs of numerous persons fill the walls. Some faces you know. Some you don't know. Who are they? Go over and gently touch the frames of the ones you love or care about. Take a moment to enjoy your memory of these persons. Thank God for the gift of these people in your life. [Pause.]

Enter the last room. It is disturbing. Scenes of destruction, pain, and neglect hang from the walls. Sculptures depict agony and despair. Look around you. . . . Take it all in. . . . These are the areas of humankind's unfaithfulness to the gifts God has given us. Sit quietly on the bench in the middle of the gallery. Think about the times in your life when you have neglected your responsibility to care for the earth and the creatures that inhabit it. . . . Think about a time when you have mistreated a pet or a time when you did not stop someone from mistreating one. . . . Think about the times you have unnecessarily acted meanly to small creatures. . . . Name those moments in which you have littered out the car window or on the beach or in the park or ball field. . . . Reflect on those situations in which you have treated persons as less than the precious creation that God fashioned. [Pause.]

Suddenly, soft footsteps approach you. Jesus is standing at the entrance of the gallery. He is very glad to see you. Hear him say your name and greet you. . . . Say hello to Jesus. . . . He comes toward you to join you on the bench. . . . Notice what you are feeling to have Jesus come in the room and sit beside you. . . .

Jesus comfortably asks you to share with him what your favorite scene in nature was. . . . Answer Jesus. Tell him about the paintings or artwork that touched you the most. [Pause.]

Jesus asks you to tell him which of the creatures are the ones that delight you or intrigue you. . . . Share with Jesus what you find awesome about God's creation. [Pause.]

Next, Jesus asks you to name those persons whom you care about. . . . He asks you to share with him how well you treat them in relationship. . . . Be honest with Jesus. [Pause.]

Finally, Jesus brings you back to focus on the disturbing paintings and statues in *this* room. Hear him ask you what painting or sculpture disturbs you the most. . . . He asks you what you can do to help. . . . He asks you to describe what you will do better to care for the gift of creation given you by your loving Creator, the Breath of All Life. . . .

Think seriously how to respond to Jesus. . . . Make yours a good solid answer. . . . Tell Jesus how you will purposefully see to your responsibility to God's earth and all creatures. [Pause.]

Jesus is pleased with you and asks you to pray with him now. He places both of his hands up in blessing toward the art that depicts such destruction. . . . He asks you to lift your hands up too. . . . Face the scene or sculpture that disturbed you the most and lift your hands up toward it. . . . Listen as Jesus prays for humanity's increased sensitivity and caring toward all of creation. . . . He prays that everyone will become more aware of his or her accountability to protect every living thing that comes from the benevolence . . . from the goodness of the Breath of All Life. . . . And Jesus prays that the heart of each person will come to know and appreciate that the Reign of God lives in creation and in each one. . . .

Jesus becomes silent. It is time now for you to add a short prayer of your own to Jesus' prayer. . . . Pray for your part in all of this. What do you pray? [Pause.]

It is time for Jesus to go now. . . . Walk him out of the room of destruction through to the other rooms. . . . [Pause.]

Finally, you stand with Jesus at the door of the art gallery. . . . Jesus gives you a good-bye hug. . . . He says your name and whispers that he loves you. . . . Notice what you are feeling to be loved by Jesus. . . .

Wander back through your favorite parts of the gallery, thinking about what you must do to care for the great beauty and resources that the Breath of All Life has given you and entrusted to you. . . .

Breathe in deeply . . . hold it . . . breathe out slowly and completely. Breathe in deeply . . . hold it . . . breathe out slowly and completely. Once more, breathe in deeply . . . hold it . . . breathe out slowly and completely. And when you are ready, you may open your eyes.

**REFLECTION** Continue playing instrumental music. Ask the participants to reflect on the experience that they have just gone through, by pondering some of the following questions, or questions similar to these. You might want to suggest that they respond to the questions that speak most personally to them. Allow time for them to write their reflections.

- What did it feel like to be in the art museum?
- In walking through the first room, containing scenes from nature, what did I choose as my favorite? Why did I choose this particular one?
- What did I say to God in thanksgiving?
- Which creatures delighted me or intrigued me as I walked through the second room? Why were these of particular interest to me?
- What did I pray to God in thanksgiving?
- Which frames did I gently touch as I walked through the room containing all the portraits and photographs of persons? Why are these persons special to me?

- Which portraits moved me? Was I surprised by any that I chose? Why or why not?
- Was it easy or difficult to lift these persons up in thanksgiving to my Creator God?
- When did I mistreat a pet or fail to stop someone else from mistreating one?
- How have I littered or neglected care for the earth?
- In what situations have I treated a person as less than a treasured creation of God?
- When I heard the footsteps in the meditation, was I glad to find that it was Jesus? Why or why not?
- How did it feel to have him sit down next to me?
- What did I tell Jesus was my favorite place in nature?
- What did Jesus say to me when I shared which creatures delighted me and intrigued me?
- How did it feel to be challenged by Jesus to take better care of the earth and those around me?
- Can I accept that I have a greater responsibility to creation than I have previously honored? If so, what will I purposefully do to see to my responsibility to God's creation?
- What do I want to remember from the prayers that Jesus and then I lifted up to the Breath of All Life?
- How did it feel to receive a hug from Jesus—to hear him say my name and that he loves me?
- Am I in a better place because of this prayer time?
- What special image or message will I remember most from this prayer experience?

Invite and encourage the participants to share their reflections, but do this without pressuring them to open up. Explain that sharing faith experiences can deepen and strengthen our faith, and that they need share only what they are comfortable disclosing to the group. Continue playing instrumental music, as it helps with reverencing the moment. Allow time for the sharing and affirming of each person.

**ART EXPRESSION AND PRAYER RITUAL (OPTIONAL)**

The art expression and prayer ritual is an optional activity. It can be used in place of the reflection questions. If you decide to use one of the activities described below, prepare the art area before the group gathers.

After the meditation, continue playing instrumental music in the art area. Invite the participants to move quietly to one of the prepared places.

**Art Expression 1**

Set a place for each participant, with magazines or newspapers, scissors, markers, a piece of construction paper, and glue. Instruct everyone to design a collage of pictures and words that express their favorite place in nature, the creatures that delight or intrigue them, and the persons whom they care about. Have them include in their artwork the destruction, pain, and neglect that have been suffered by the earth and God's creatures, including human beings. Finally, ask them to include their personal plan of how they will care for God's creation more intentionally.

**Art Expression 2**

Set a place for each participant, with a sheet of art paper, a ruler, a pencil or pen, and crayons or markers. Instruct the participants to draw a frame around the edge of their art paper and then to summarize what they will remember most from this prayer experience and write it inside the frame. Next, invite them to draw the artwork in the museum that moved them the most or represented their favorite part of creation.

After either art project, explain that sharing our faith experiences can help strengthen our faith. Then invite the participants to share the effect the prayer time had on them, by explaining the symbolism of their collage or drawing. Suggest that after they have finished describing their artwork, they lift it high and say, "Creator God, Breath of All Life, thank you," or something similar before placing their art in the middle of the prayer circle or in another designated area. Provide ample time for the sharing and affirming of each person. Continue playing instrumental music, as it helps with reverencing the moment.

Remind the participants that they can return to their imagination at any time and be with Jesus to talk about anything. Encourage them to place their art expression in a visible spot in their home to remind them of their responsibility to all of creation.

**CLOSING**

For closure to the meditation experience, read aloud the following litany of thanksgiving:

> *Litany Response*
> Creator God, Breath of All Life, thank you for your gifts.
>
> In the sea . . . with its whales, dolphins, turtles, coral, oysters, fish, seals, seaweed, and shellfish . . . [All respond.]
>
> In the sky . . . with its rainbows, clouds, gulls, herons, canaries, hawks, eagles, sparrows, butterflies, and hummingbirds . . . [All respond.]
>
> In the human heart of my neighbor . . . with its potentiality, love, forgiveness, mercy, faith, hope, generosity, and gentleness . . . [All respond.]
>
> On land . . . with its alligators, elk, elephants, trees, mountains, valleys, rain forests, ants, inchworms, and bullfrogs . . . [All respond.]
>
> In the universe . . . with its stars, sun, moon, planets, meteors, asteroids, and comets . . . [All respond.]
>
> For our pets . . . our gerbils, ferrets, dogs, cats, hamsters, horses, mice, snakes, and rabbits . . . [All respond.]
>
> For exotic birds, animals, and plants . . . the flamingos, peacocks, lemurs, white elephants, lady's slippers, and orchids . . . [All respond.]

The participants may each be invited to name one of their favorite gifts of creation that hasn't yet been expressed, and then all may join in the response once more to close.

# *Kingdom Now*
# *The Spirit of the Lord Has Sent Me*

This enlightening prayer experience, "The Spirit of the Lord Has Sent Me," is based on the passage from Luke in which Jesus stands up and reads the words of the prophet Isaiah from the scroll. Emphatically, Jesus acknowledges the Spirit as having sent him. It reminds us that the Spirit of the Lord sends us as well, and we must be about the business of building the Kingdom now.

**THEME** After you have given directions to the participants and set the tone for meditation, introduce the theme by saying something like the following:

> So often we fail to connect with the power of the Spirit; yet it was the same Spirit that Jesus acknowledged when he stood up in the Temple to read from the Scriptures. It was the same Spirit that Jesus left to his Apostles and to all who follow him. It is the same Spirit that yearns to burn in the hearts of all of us, so that we might reach out to the poor, the blind, the oppressed, the sick, and the imprisoned, and clearly demonstrate that the Reign of God is present on earth. If we allow ourselves to enter our quiet place apart, then we can discover how the Spirit of the Lord sends us.

**OPENING** Read aloud this opening prayer:

> Spirit of the Living God, you have been with us since the beginning of time. Jesus assured us again of your real and steadfast presence when he made known to the Apostles who you are as helper and guide. Open our hearts this day so that we might connect with you in a

> powerful way and thereby help to bring about the Kingdom now among your people. Grace us with courage, willingness, and a strong faith, so that we may unselfishly act as Jesus did in his relationships with the poor, the blind, the sick, the oppressed, and the imprisoned. Help us to be a vehicle through which others personally experience the Reign of God as present among us. We ask all this with trust in your powerful presence and loving guidance. Amen.

**SCRIPTURE** Read aloud Luke 4:16–21, using a Bible.

**SCRIPT** Play "The Spirit of the Lord Has Sent Me" meditation on the accompanying recording, or slowly and reverently read aloud the following script for the guided meditation. Play soft, instrumental background music.

> Today you will enter the hush of your quiet place and meet Jesus in your imagination. First, you will begin by doing some deep-breathing exercises. When I say to, if you can, breathe in and out through your nose very quietly during these exercises. Close your eyes and get comfortable. You will be relaxing your entire body.
>
> Breathe in deeply . . . hold it . . . breathe out slowly and completely. Breathe in deeply . . . hold it . . . breathe out slowly and completely. Again, breathe in deeply . . . hold it . . . breathe out slowly and completely.
>
> Allow your feet and ankles to relax. . . . Relax your legs . . . and your hips. . . . Stay mindful of your breathing. Relax your stomach muscles . . . and now your chest. . . . Just relax. . . . Let your arms grow limp. . . . Relax your wrists, . . . your hands, . . . and your fingers. . . . Keep breathing in deeply and out slowly.

Allow your shoulders to become heavy. . . . Let all the tension drain from your shoulders. . . . Relax your neck, . . . your facial muscles, . . . your forehead, . . . and even your eyelids. . . . Just relax. . . . Breathe in deeply . . . hold it . . . breathe out slowly and completely. [Pause.]

You are in the Temple among the crowd that has just finished hearing Jesus proclaim the words of Isaiah. It was a powerful reading by Jesus. He was sure about what he was saying. His face glowed. He wanted everyone to hear—to believe—that the Spirit of the Lord had sent him . . . that he was to fulfill the words of Isaiah.

You leave the Temple and walk out into the Temple courtyard with the crowd. . . . You hear your name called out. . . . At least, you think you do. You turn but don't see anyone looking for you. . . . You keep walking. . . . You think about the words Jesus read . . . how he was to bring good news to the poor, sight to the blind, and freedom to the oppressed. . . . It is a lot to think about. Again, you believe you hear your name being called. . . . You turn to see if there is someone. Jesus is hurrying after you! . . . You! He is moving through the crowd of people to catch up with you. Again, he calls your name . . . and calls for you to wait up.

He seems pleased to have caught up with you. He greets you warmly with a brief touch on your shoulder. . . . Notice what you are feeling to be sought by Jesus. . . . He asks you to take a walk with him. . . . Lovingly he asks, "Can we talk? . . ."

Begin to walk with Jesus and listen as he tells you that he knows that you carry heavy stuff in your heart . . . that there are things that you are not proud of . . . that there are relationships that could be more loving . . . and that there are areas in your life in which you would like to grow. . . . Hear Jesus invite you to tell him all about this stuff in your heart. . . . He wants to carry it with you. . . . Take this time to tell him everything. [Pause.]

Jesus asks you to choose people and things and situations that are better for you . . . and can you do this? . . . Answer Jesus. . . .

He asks you to remember to call upon the Spirit to lead you, . . . and he also challenges you to go beyond yourself and help others. . . . He tells you that the words of the prophet Isaiah are for you . . . that you must bring Good News to the poor, . . . help those who are blinded, . . . and offer freedom to those who are held captive by stuff in their lives, . . . who are oppressed in some way. . . . Hear him as he tells you that he believes in you and in your personal part in building the Kingdom now. . . . Notice what you are feeling to hear this. . . .

Jesus asks you to name anyone whom you know who may be blind . . . blind to their own goodness and worth . . . blind to the love from others . . . blind to the needs of others . . . or blind physically. . . . Tell Jesus about anyone whom you think fits this category and talk about how you might help them. [Pause.]

Now share with Jesus those persons whom you can reach out to who are prisoners of their own self-doubt, inner pain or secrets, fears, or addictions. Take your time and think of anyone that this describes and then tell Jesus whom you might help and how. [Pause.]

Jesus asks you to reflect on your attitude toward the poor . . . those who are financially poor, . . . those who are poor emotionally because they have lost hope, . . . and those who are poor because they have no friends or support. . . . He checks in with you about how you might bring good news and hope to these poor. . . . Answer Jesus. [Pause.]

He reminds you that the Spirit has been given to you . . . that the Spirit is the life-giving power behind all your actions of love and courage and acceptance. . . . He prays that you will call on his Spirit freely and often. . . . Jesus takes both your hands in his. . . . He says your name and blesses you with love. [Pause.]

Jesus tells you he must leave you now. . . . Thank Jesus for this time together. . . . And say your good-byes in whatever way expresses how you are feeling. [Pause.]

Watch as Jesus walks back toward the Temple area. . . . He turns to wave to you, which makes you feel good. . . . Continue walking and reflect on all that you have talked about . . . about how Jesus told you that the Spirit of the Lord has sent you . . . you! . . . and that there are people that you need to reach out to . . . and that because of you they will experience the Kingdom of God as present on earth now. You can do this. . . . Jesus is counting on you . . . for the Spirit of the Lord has sent you. . . . [Pause.]

Breathe in deeply . . . hold it . . . breathe out slowly and completely. Breathe in deeply . . . hold it . . . breathe out slowly and completely. Once more, breathe in deeply . . . hold it . . . breathe out slowly and completely. And when you are ready, you may open your eyes.

**REFLECTION** Continue playing instrumental music. Ask the participants to reflect on the experience that they have just gone through, by pondering some of the following questions, or questions similar to these. You might want to suggest that they respond to the questions that speak most personally to them. Allow time for them to write their reflections.

- What was it like for me to be in the Temple area with the crowd who had heard Jesus proclaim the words of the prophet Isaiah?
- What did I think when I thought I heard someone call my name?
- How did I feel when I realized it was Jesus calling to me and hurrying after me? What was it like to be invited to take a walk and talk with Jesus?
- What things that I am not proud of did I tell Jesus about?
- What relationships did I tell Jesus that I could be more loving in?
- What did I share with Jesus as the areas in my life in which I need to grow?
- What, if any, additional heavy stuff in my heart did I confide in Jesus? How did it feel to unburden myself to Jesus?
- When Jesus asked me to choose people, things, or situations that were better for me, how did I respond to him?
- Whom did I name that may be blind
    - to their own goodness and worth?
    - to love from others?
    - to the needs of others?
    - physically?
- What did I tell Jesus regarding how I might help those whom I named as blind?
- Whom did I name who are prisoners
    - of their own self-doubt?
    - of inner pain or secrets?
    - of fears?
    - of addictions?
- What did I tell Jesus as to how I might help anyone whom I have named as a prisoner?

- What is my attitude toward
  - the financially poor?
  - the emotionally poor who have lost hope?
  - the relationally poor who have no friends or support?
- What did I tell Jesus as to how I might bring the Good News and hope to the poor?
- What did I think or feel when Jesus reminded me that the Spirit of the Lord has been given to me?
- What were my emotions when Jesus took both of my hands in his, said my name, and blessed me?
- Do I now believe more fully that the Spirit of the Lord has sent me? Am I more aware that Jesus is counting on me to make the Reign of God present to others? If so, what will I do first to begin living out this responsibility?
- What was it like saying good-bye to Jesus? How did I feel when he turned and waved to me one more time?
- What special message or image will I remember most from this prayer experience?

Invite and encourage the participants to share their reflections, but do this without pressuring them to open up. Explain that sharing faith experiences can deepen and strengthen our faith, and that they need share only what they are comfortable disclosing to the group. Continue playing instrumental music, as it helps with reverencing the moment. Allow time for the sharing and affirming of each person.

**ART EXPRESSION AND PRAYER RITUAL (OPTIONAL)**

The art expression and prayer ritual is an optional activity. It can be used in place of the reflection questions. If you decide to use one of the activities described below, prepare the art area before the group gathers.

After the meditation, continue playing instrumental music in the art area. Invite the participants to move quietly to one of the prepared places.

**Art Expression 1**

Set a place for each participant, with one piece of white or manila art paper, pieces of construction or tissue paper in various colors, and glue. Direct the participants to tear strips and shapes out of the construction or tissue paper, using the shapes and colors to symbolize people they know who are blind, imprisoned, or poor in some way. Instruct them to use additional colors and shapes to represent their own plan of action to help these people. Have them arrange the shapes and strips on the art paper in collage fashion and then glue them down.

*Alternative approach.* Using the same materials, invite the participants to use colors and shapes that symbolize the ways they see *themselves* as blind, imprisoned, or poor. Instruct them to use additional colors and shapes to symbolize their plan of action to deal with these areas in their own life—for example, whom they might turn to or what they might do differently.

**Art Expression 2** Set a place for each participant, with a large sheet of art or poster paper, crayons or markers, a pen or pencil, a scissors, glue, and magazines or newspapers. Direct the participants to cut out articles, words, and photographs that represent persons who are in some way blind, imprisoned, or poor. Instruct them to make a collage of the words, articles, and photos that they have chosen and to glue them on the large art or poster paper. Tell them to leave space to write about how they will help the blind, the imprisoned, or the poor whom they have represented. Advise them to use markers or crayons to highlight certain articles or pictures or merely to make their poster more colorful.

After either art project, explain that sharing our faith experiences can help strengthen our faith. Then invite the participants to share the effect the prayer time had on them, by explaining the significance of the colors, words, or symbols expressed in their artwork. Add that after they have finished describing their artwork, they are to reverently lift it high and say, "The Spirit of the Lord has sent me," or something similar before placing their art in the middle of the prayer circle or another designated area. Provide ample time for the sharing and affirming of each person. Continue playing instrumental music, as it helps with reverencing the moment.

Remind the participants that they can return to their imagination at any time and meet Jesus, who will always be there to remind them that the Spirit sends them as the Spirit sent him. Encourage them to place their art expression in a visible spot in their home as a reminder of their time spent with Jesus and of how they will live out their compassion and response to the blind, the imprisoned, and the poor.

**CLOSING** For closure to the meditation experience, have different participants share in reading aloud the following litany of petition:

> *Litany Response*
> Spirit of the Living God, guide us.
>
> When we can help someone held captive by their own self-doubts, we pray . . . [All respond.]
>
> When we become aware of somebody's struggle with an addiction, we pray . . . [All respond.]
>
> In those moments when we don't know what to say, we pray . . . [All respond.]
>
> For the opportunities that place us in the presence of those who are imprisoned by their own fears or built-up walls, we pray . . . [All respond.]
>
> In situations where we can help others remove their blindfolds of apathy or low self-esteem, we pray . . . [All respond.]
>
> When we might ease somebody's burden by listening attentively, we pray . . . [All respond.]

For the times when we are uncomfortable and want to turn away from another person's disability, whether physical, emotional, or mental, we pray . . . [All respond.]

For situations where we are faced with another's financial poverty, loss of hope, or lack of support or friendship, we pray . . . [All respond.]

When we carry around our own blindness, oppression, and poverty, we pray . . . [All respond.]

# *Sharing Everything in Common*

This challenging prayer experience, "Everything in Common," is based on the passage in the Acts of the Apostles in which it is clearly noted that true disciples of Jesus shared everything. It reminds us that we have a Christian obligation to serve and care for others in the same loving and thoughtful ways as did the early disciples.

**THEME** After you have given directions to the participants and set the tone for meditation, introduce the theme by saying something like the following:

> We live in a self-centered society. We're taught to take care of ourselves, and we're told that justice is more about how we are treated than about how we treat others. We collect innumerable possessions that we cannot possibly do without, while our brothers and sisters in inner cities and in poverty-stricken nations throughout the world barely survive. There must be some way that we can respond. If we are open to entering our quiet place apart, we can allow ourselves to be honestly challenged to find ways that we can share more with others.

**OPENING** Read aloud this opening prayer:

> Jesus, the early communities of your followers demonstrated the love you showed them by sharing everything in common. No one went without. Please come to us in our quiet place apart so that we might honestly look at the ways we continue to be selfish. Grant us the creative openness to explore ways we can reach out more delib-

erately with the loving and thoughtful attitudes of your first disciples. Grace us with the courage to be generous and to put others first. We lift this prayer up to you with sincerity of heart. Amen.

**SCRIPTURE** Read aloud Acts of the Apostles 2:42–47, using a Bible.

**SCRIPT** Play the "Everything in Common" meditation on the accompanying recording, or slowly and reverently read aloud the following script for the guided meditation. Play soft, instrumental background music.

Today you will enter the hush of your quiet place and meet Jesus in your imagination. First, you will begin by doing some deep-breathing exercises. When I say to, if you can, breathe in and out through your nose very quietly during these exercises. Close your eyes and get comfortable. You will be relaxing your entire body.

Breathe in deeply . . . hold it . . . breathe out slowly and completely. Breathe in deeply . . . hold it . . . breathe out slowly and completely. Again, breathe in deeply . . . hold it . . . breathe out slowly and completely.

Allow your feet and ankles to relax. . . . Relax your legs . . . and your hips. . . . Stay mindful of your breathing. Relax your stomach muscles . . . and now your chest. . . . Just relax. . . . Let your arms grow limp. . . . Relax your wrists, . . . your hands, . . . and your fingers. . . . Keep breathing in deeply and out slowly.

Allow your shoulders to become heavy. . . . Let all the tension drain from your shoulders. . . . Relax your neck, . . . your facial muscles, . . . your forehead, . . . and even your eyelids. . . . Just relax. . . . Breathe in deeply . . . hold it . . . breathe out slowly and completely. [Pause.]

Today you are safely alone and riding on a slowly moving train. The day is lovely and the sky is clear. . . . At first you see only scenery outside. Take a moment to enjoy it.

But as you continue to watch out your window, you notice scenes from your life passing by. They are scenes that show you as loving and caring about others. Perhaps you are reaching out to and accepting someone who is different . . . or you are being kind to someone disabled. . . . Perhaps you are being thoughtful to a family member . . . or are sharing your money or food with someone who needs it. . . . Perhaps it is a moment of volunteer service . . . or you are going through your clothes or possessions to donate to the needy. . . . Perhaps you are including someone in a project or an outing for which you had to push yourself to make it happen. . . . Perhaps you are being a good listener to someone with a problem. . . . No matter what the scenes, just watch and appreciate who you are at your best and loving self. [Pause.]

Now the scenes of your life are changing. Be prepared. These scenes depict the moments when you were uncaring or selfish. . . . Watch as the scenes roll by you. . . . Notice what you are feeling to watch yourself in your less favorable moments. [Pause.]

The scenes outside your window return to nature. . . . It is time for some soul-searching. . . . Think about any possessions that you may have two of. . . . Can you offer one up for someone else? . . . Can you donate more money than you have in the past to the needy? . . . When you go to the mall or supermarket, could you consider buying something for a stranger in a shelter? . . . Can you drop off or mail a donation of some sort to a teen shelter or a battered women's shelter, a residence for AIDS patients, or an inner-city school? . . . Have you ever thought to join with your friends or family members to start a club and reach out to others? . . . Reflect on these possibilities or others that would help you to be as sincere and as giving as the early disciples . . . sharing everything in common. What could you really do? Think about it. [Pause.]

There is a slight rustling as the door of your train opens. Don't be afraid. It is Jesus. He has come to discuss things with you. He wants to talk to you about sharing. Hear him greet you by name. . . . He smiles at you and sits opposite you. . . . Greet Jesus. . . . [Pause.]

Jesus seems comfortable to be with you and leans toward you and asks you to share with him one of your life scenes that you witnessed out the train window that you were proud of. . . . Tell Jesus . . . and then allow him to tell you how pleased he is with you when you are your best self. [Pause.]

Jesus asks you to let him know which scenes bothered you the most when what you saw out your window depicted you as uncaring or self-centered. . . . Use this special time between you and Jesus to talk about your selfishness . . . where that might come from . . . and why sometimes it might get the better of you. . . . Go ahead, talk with Jesus about these times when you are not your best self. [Pause.]

Tell Jesus that you are sorry for those times . . . and hear Jesus forgive you. [Pause.]

Jesus challenges you to thoughtfully reflect on what you might do to grow in generosity. . . . He asks you what it is that you can really choose to do . . . what you will commit to doing in order to share the goods you possess . . . both the goods that come from within you and the goods that are your possessions, money, talent, or ability to help. . . . What can you really choose to do? Answer Jesus and truly commit to what you tell him. [Pause.]

Jesus is pleased. . . . He tells you that the Reign of God will be more evident because of your caring and giving. . . . Jesus blesses you. . . . Allow yourself to feel this special moment between you and Jesus. [Pause.]

Jesus gets up to leave you. . . . He smiles at you, says your name with such warmth, and, "I love you. . . ." Tell Jesus what you need to before he leaves. [Pause.]

Remain quiet after Jesus departs . . . and think about your intended ways of sharing more generously, . . . for you desire to be like the early disciples, doing your best to be observant of other's needs and by sharing everything in common. . . .

Breathe in deeply . . . hold it . . . breathe out slowly and completely. Breathe in deeply . . . hold it . . . breathe out slowly and completely. Once more, breathe in deeply . . . hold it . . . breathe out slowly and completely. And when you are ready, you may open your eyes.

**REFLECTION** Continue playing instrumental music. Ask the participants to reflect on the experience that they have just gone through, by pondering some of the following questions, or questions similar to these. You might want to suggest that they respond to the questions that speak most personally to them. Allow time for them to write their reflections.

- What did I notice when the first nature scenes passed by? How was I feeling?
- What was it like for me to sit alone on the train and watch scenes from my life in which I was loving, thoughtful, and kind?
- Is there one scene that I am more proud of than others? Why?
- What scenes depicted me as selfish and uncaring?
- How did those scenes make me feel?
- Is there one scene that I am less proud of than others? If so, why?
- Could I think of any possessions of which I own two that I could offer one up for someone else? If so, what are they? Is there anything else that I could part with so that someone else might have it? If so, what is it?
- Could I donate more money than I have in the past to share with the needy? If so, what is my plan?
- Can I purposefully go to the market or mall the next time and buy something for a stranger in a shelter? If so, what should I purchase?
- What other donation might I make to a teen shelter, a battered women's shelter, a residence for AIDS patients, or an inner-city school? When will I follow up and do this?
- Am I moved to start a club or project with family or friends to reach out to others? If so, whom would I like to serve, and who could I ask to help me? If not, why don't I think I could do this?
- What did I share with Jesus about a time when I was my best self? How did I feel sharing that with Jesus? What did Jesus say in response to me?
- What scene of selfishness did I share with Jesus? Can I avoid being selfish the next time I am faced with the same situation? Comment.
- How did it feel for me to tell Jesus that I was sorry? Could I allow myself to experience Jesus' forgiveness? Why or why not?

- When Jesus asked me to name what I will do to grow in generosity, what did I tell him? Am I truly committed to doing this? Why or why not?
- Do I believe that the Reign of God will be more evident because of my caring and giving? Why or why not?
- What did I think when Jesus blessed me? How did I feel?
- How will I try to keep conscious the need to "share everything in common"? What will I do first?
- What is the most special message or image that I will remember from this prayer experience?

Invite and encourage the participants to share their reflections, but do this without pressuring them to open up. Explain that sharing faith experiences can deepen and strengthen our faith, and that they need share only what they are comfortable disclosing to the group. Continue playing instrumental music, as it helps with reverencing the moment. Allow time for the sharing and affirming of each person.

**ART EXPRESSION AND PRAYER RITUAL (OPTIONAL)**

The art expression and prayer ritual is an optional activity. It can be used in place of the reflection questions. If you decide to use one of the activities described below, prepare the art area before the group gathers.

After the meditation, continue playing instrumental music in the art area. Invite the participants to move quietly to one of the prepared places.

**Art Expression 1**

Set a place for each participant, with one piece of colored construction paper, a slightly smaller sheet of white paper, crayons or markers, and a pen. Have glue or glue sticks available.

Instruct the participants to divide their white paper into blocks and then draw in the blocks some of the scenes they saw outside the train window. Encourage them to depict a moment or two when they were their best selves and a moment or two when they were selfish and uncaring. Direct them to draw another scene that expresses their plan to share more generously. Have them glue their page of scenes to the colored construction paper.

**Art Expression 2** Set a place for each participant, with a 3-inch heart cut from heavy construction paper or poster board. Add markers, crayons, a scissors, and three 8-inch pieces of yarn. Have available a laminating machine or clear contact paper, and a paper punch.

Instruct the participants to design a heart-shaped bookmark with the most important message they received from their prayer experience. Direct them to laminate the bookmark or cover it with clear contact paper, trim the edges, and punch a hole at the top. Then have them thread the three pieces of yarn through the hole and make a tassel.

**Art Expression 3** Set a place for each participant, with stationery, a pen, and a stamped envelope. Instruct the participants to write a letter to themselves from Jesus. Invite them to highlight things they need to remember about the times when they were their best selves and the times when they were selfish or uncaring. Direct them to include the plan that they talked about with Jesus—the plan to be like his disciples and share everything in common, the plan to be more generous. Ask them to address the envelope to themselves. After the sharing, have them seal their envelope. Collect the letters at the end of the session and mail them to the participants in a week or so as a reminder of their commitment to do better in their generosity and caring for others.

After any of these art projects, explain that sharing our faith experiences can help strengthen our faith. Then invite the participants to share the effect the prayer time had on them, by explaining the significance of their drawings, bookmark, or letter. Add that after they have finished describing their artwork, they are to place it on the altar, in the prayer circle, or in another designated spot. As they place their artwork, they are to pray, "Jesus, help me to be a true disciple and share what I have," or something similar. Provide ample time for the sharing and affirming of each person. Continue playing instrumental music, as it helps with reverencing the moment.

Remind the participants that they can return to their imagination at any time and be in the presence of the Holy One. Encourage them to place their art expression in a visible spot in their home as a reminder of their commitment to try "sharing everything in common." If art expression 3 was chosen, recommend that when they receive their letter, they examine their progress in sharing more generously. Suggest that they then keep their letter in a place where they will come across it often.

**CLOSING** For closure to the meditation experience, lead the following litany of petition:

> *Litany Response*
> Give us a sharing heart, O God.
>
> When we forget that others may not have life as easy as we do . . . [All respond.]
>
> When we fail to recognize that all are our sisters and brothers . . . [All respond.]
>
> When we do wrong by giving in to our selfishness and pride . . . [All respond.]
>
> When we devalue someone because of their economic status, their nondesigner clothes, or their possessions that are not new or in style . . . [All respond.]
>
> When we disappoint other people by not loving generously, help us make it up to them and . . . [All respond.]
>
> When we're stubborn or narrow-minded and think we have to have it all to be popular . . . [All respond.]
>
> When we're hesitant to reach out and answer someone else's need . . . [All respond.]

When we have more than enough, or a possession we don't need or use . . . [All respond.]

When we could stretch during the times we have little, and give to another . . . [All respond.]

When time, talent, or energy is all that we can give . . . [All respond.]

# *New Jerusalem*
# *God's Name on Your Forehead*

This empowering prayer experience, "God's Name on Your Forehead," is based on a Scripture passage in the Book of Revelation, which describes the author's vision of the New Jerusalem . . . the place of eternal life that we know as heaven. It reminds us that we need to put things in right order so that heaven may one day be ours.

**THEME** After you have given directions to the participants and set the tone for meditation, introduce the theme by saying something like the following:

> Often we aren't even thinking about the end of our life. We are too busy living it. Yet the message in Revelation is important. We must put things in right order if we want to "bear God's name on our forehead," if we want to live in the place where every tear will be wiped away, if we want eternal life with God. If we allow ourselves to enter our quiet place apart, then we will be able to examine honestly the things in our life that we need to put in right order.

**OPENING** Read aloud this opening prayer:

> Eternal God, grace us with the power of your presence as we examine the things that we must put in right order. Grant us the honesty to look into all the shadows that we sometimes avoid, those character flaws and bad habits that we are not proud of. We pray that through this prayer experience, we will be empowered to make the necessary changes so that we might bear your name on our forehead and enter the New Jerusalem for all

eternity. We lift this prayer up to you and say . . . amen.

**SCRIPTURE** Read aloud Revelation 21:1—22:5, using a Bible.

**SCRIPT** Play the "God's Name on Your Forehead" meditation on the accompanying recording, or slowly and reverently read aloud the following script for the guided meditation. Play soft, instrumental background music.

Today you will enter the hush of your quiet place and meet Jesus in your imagination. First, you will begin by doing some deep-breathing exercises. When I say to, if you can, breathe in and out through your nose very quietly during these exercises. Close your eyes and get comfortable. You will be relaxing your entire body.

Breathe in deeply . . . hold it . . . breathe out slowly and completely. Breathe in deeply . . . hold it . . . breathe out slowly and completely. Again, breathe in deeply . . . hold it . . . breathe out slowly and completely.

Allow your feet and ankles to relax. . . . Relax your legs . . . and your hips. . . . Stay mindful of your breathing. Relax your stomach muscles . . . and now your chest. . . . Just relax. . . . Let your arms grow limp. . . . Relax your wrists, . . . your hands, . . . and your fingers. . . . Keep breathing in deeply and out slowly.

Allow your shoulders to become heavy. . . . Let all the tension drain from your shoulders. . . . Relax your neck, . . . your facial muscles, . . . your forehead, . . . and even your eyelids. . . . Just relax. . . . Breathe in deeply . . . hold it . . . breathe out slowly and completely. [Pause.]

You are standing at the gates of heaven. . . . It can look like anything you would like it to. . . . Take a moment to look all around you. . . . It is beautiful. . . . It gives you a sense of true, internal peace. . . . You hear music. . . . There is a bright warmth illuminating from the gates. . . . Immediately, Jesus comes through them to stand by you. . . . He has such joy on his face. . . . He greets you by name . . . and tells you how happy he is to have this special time with you. . . .

Together you find a place to sit down. . . . Jesus tells you that heaven with him is what your whole life's journey is toward. . . . He tells you that those who enter here will have God's name on their foreheads . . . they will be known by the love that they share. . . . He tells you that here every tear will be wiped away. . . . Notice what you are feeling when you hear this. . . . With love and compassion, Jesus asks you to share your deepest pain. . . . Allow yourself to feel free to tell Jesus everything and anything. He wants to hold it with you. Talk to him now. [Pause.]

Listen as Jesus responds to what you have shared. There is so much love in his voice. [Pause.]

Jesus now gently reminds you that you must work on putting everything in right order . . . everything that you are capable of. . . . Hear him first ask you about the people in your life. . . . He asks you to name those whom you must treat more kindly and those whom you need to let go of so as to live a more wholesome and holy life. . . . Take this time to talk with Jesus about the people in your life. [Pause.]

Next, Jesus asks you to name any of your habits or character flaws, your temper, or negative attitudes that you need to work on. . . . Take this time to give these all over to Jesus. He will work on them with you. [Pause.]

Jesus now softly says, "Tell me any situations or things that you are involved in in which you need to make different decisions. . . . I will help you to put these things in right order . . . if you let me. . . ." Go ahead. This is the time to do it. . . . Share with Jesus anything that you need help with. [Pause.]

You and Jesus now make a plan to put in right order many of the things that you have shared with him. . . . Allow yourself to feel empowered as you and Jesus work on your plan together. [Pause.]

Feel Jesus' two warm, strong, but gentle hands as he lays them on your head in blessing. . . . He prays for your courage until the day you will be with him forever. . . . He prays for God's name on your forehead. Listen as he prays. [Pause.]

It is time to say good-bye. Do so in whatever way is comfortable for you. . . . You watch as Jesus walks back to enter the gate. . . . Think about this time you have shared together. . . . Think about the things that you have to put in right order . . . for you want to enter the New Jerusalem with God's name on your forehead. . . .

Breathe in deeply . . . hold it . . . breathe out slowly and completely. Breathe in deeply . . . hold it . . . breathe out slowly and completely. Once more, breathe in deeply . . . hold it . . . breathe out slowly and completely. And when you are ready, you may open your eyes.

**REFLECTION** Continue playing instrumental music. Ask the participants to reflect on the experience that they have just gone through, by pondering some of the following questions, or questions similar to these. You might want to suggest that they respond to the questions that speak most personally to them. Allow time for them to write their reflections.

- How did I picture heaven?
- What was my reaction to being there?
- When Jesus approached me, greeting me by name and telling me he was happy to have special time with me, how did it make me feel?
- What were my thoughts when Jesus said that those who enter heaven will have God's name on their forehead? Did I think that God's name would be on my forehead? Why or why not?
- What was the deep pain that I shared with Jesus? How did it feel to share it with him?
- What did I tell Jesus that I had to put in right order regarding
  - people whom I must treat more kindly?
  - people whom I need to let go of so that I can have a more wholesome and holy life?
  - other people?
- What habits, character flaws, or negative attitudes did I tell Jesus I need to work on? Did I also mention my temper?
- What situations or things in which I'm involved do I need to make different decisions about?
- What is the plan Jesus and I developed to put these things in right order?
- What emotion was stirred in me when Jesus placed his two gentle hands on my head in blessing?
- What was it like for me to hear Jesus' prayer of courage for me, to hear his prayer that God's name be on my forehead?
- In what way did Jesus and I say good-bye to each other? How did I feel when Jesus left?
- Am I empowered by Jesus to put in right order the dark, painful parts of my life? If so, what is the first relationship, thing, or situation that I will work on? If not, what else do I need to motivate me to put all in right order?

- Do I believe that I can attain "God's name on my forehead"? How important is this goal to me? How will I get the help I need to succeed?
- What message or image that will I remember most from this prayer experience?

Invite and encourage the participants to share their reflections, but do this without pressuring them to open up. Explain that sharing faith experiences can deepen and strengthen our faith, and that they need share only what they are comfortable disclosing to the group. Continue playing instrumental music, as it helps with reverencing the moment. Allow time for the sharing and affirming of each person.

## ART EXPRESSION AND PRAYER RITUAL (OPTIONAL)

The art expression and prayer ritual is an optional activity. It can be used in place of the reflection questions. If you decide to use one of the activities described below, prepare the art area before the group gathers.

After the meditation, continue playing instrumental music in the art area. Invite the participants to move quietly to one of the prepared places.

### Art Expression 1

Set a place for each participant, with a sheet of white drawing paper, fine-point markers or pens, and crayons or colored pencils. Direct the participants to fold their paper so that it has either four columns or four blocks. Ask them to write in the first section the relationships that they must put in right order; in the second, their character flaws, temper, negative attitudes, or habits that need work; in the third, the situations or things in which they are involved that require them to make different decisions. Finally, in the fourth section, invite them to write their plan to put these relationships, situations, or things in right order. Next, instruct them to choose for each section a color that symbolizes how they feel about what is written there and to use that color to shade in the area. Encourage them to use their artwork to express what the prayer experience has meant to them.

**Art Expression 2** Set a place for each participant, with newspaper, a sheet of art paper, watercolors, a paintbrush, a bowl of water, and paper towels. Instruct the participants to paint a scene from their meditation and to indicate through colors, symbols, or words what their time with Jesus meant to them. Invite them to use their painting to reveal how they will put things in right order so as to bear God's name on their forehead.

After either art project, explain that sharing our faith experiences can help strengthen our faith. Then invite the participants to share the effect the prayer time had on them, by explaining the colors, scene, or symbolism of their artwork. Add that after they have finished describing their art expression, perhaps they could pray, "Jesus, help me to put things in right order," or "God, I want your name on my forehead," or something similar as they place their artwork in the middle of the prayer circle or some other designated place. Provide ample time for the sharing and affirming of each person. Continue playing instrumental music, as it helps with reverencing the moment.

Remind the participants that they can return to their imagination at any time and be with Jesus in this real way. Suggest that they place their artwork in a visible spot in their home to remind them that their goal is to bear God's name on their forehead so that they can enter the New Jerusalem.

**CLOSING** For closure to the meditation experience, lead the following litany of petition:

> *Litany Response*
> God, help us to bear your name on our forehead.
>
> For the times when we are tempted to engage in immoral activity that hurts ourselves and one another . . . [All respond.]
>
> For unhealthy relationships that need to be let go of, give us courage and . . . [All respond.]

> For the times when our temper, negative attitudes, habits, or character flaws want to overpower us . . . [All respond.]
>
> For the moments in which we could be kinder to those in our path . . . [All respond.]
>
> For the areas of our life in which we need to make different decisions . . . [All respond.]
>
> For the circumstances in which we could stand firm and truly act as your child of the New Jerusalem . . . [All respond.]

Invite the participants to add any other prayer intentions. When all have finished, close by praying once more, "God, help us to bear your name on our forehead."

**ACKNOWLEDGMENTS**
*(continued from page 4)*

With eternal gratitude to Barry Russo, the musician whose talented gift sets the tone for those who pray these meditations . . . you are blessing.

To Anthony Marrapese, of Reel to Real Recording Studio, Cranston, Rhode Island, much appreciation for the fun yet exactness of our recording sessions . . . you're the best!

Many thanks to Brian Singer-Towns, my new editor, for adopting me at the retiring of my wonderful long-time editor, Fr. Bob Stamschror . . . kudos to your whole team.

And always love to those of you who mirror the Reign of God at hand: Isabel, Shirley, Aggie, Jean, Eileen, Cheryl, Bob, Bren, Alycia, Terri, Jude, Marlene, Claire, Junie, Donna, Lorraine, and my own Drea, Andre, Tom, Shaun, Mom and Dad, and clan. Bless you. . . .